# SELF-LOVE REVOLUTION

# SELF-LOVE REVOLUTION

## *Embrace Your True Worth*

CARMEN WILDE

QuillQuest Publishers

# CONTENTS

# CHAPTER 1

# Introduction

It's time to revolutionize your world with your own inner revolution. Embrace your true worth. The main goal of the self-love revolution is to help you learn how to accept self-love. Do you keep yourself busy either obsessing over someone or something, even with emotions such as worry, joy, anger, or fear? Perhaps worrying about all the things that could possibly go wrong, and looking for answers and problems solidarity. Wouldn't it be better if you just relaxed and noticed the absolute beauty behind the moment? If you are willing to heal, I could show you a freedom that has no explanation. I want to share the insurmountable peace that lives and comes with acceptance of love. I want to help you embrace the excitement to an accomplished life filled with meaningful connections. Welcome to the self-love revolution, where I encourage you to emancipate anything that makes you feel indifferent, and speak about the wonder of who you really are!

You are worthy of love and respect (in fact, it's impossible to get your life working until you completely accept that idea). Once you embrace your own worth, other things fall into place. The book's main purpose is to help you embrace and demonstrate self-love.

Regardless of what your self-esteem issues are – perhaps you self-sabotage to keep emotional distance with what feels safe and known, perhaps you have a fear of responsibility or intimacy, or you don't feel deserving, or you overwork – you must understand one thing about yourself: you are a loving and beautiful person who deserves to have a supportive, fun, intimate life full of meaningful connections. This book will help you learn how to accept self-love grace.

# CHAPTER 2

# Understanding Self-Love

Jayne was a high pastry chef in New York City. Everyone she knew liked her creativity, mastery, and teaching skills. However, she had suffered from depression and had tried to suffocate herself by drinking and experimenting with drugs. The first step to helping her heal was to help her realize one thing that each of us must recognize: A lack of self-love led us to take actions that demonstrate our personal quest for healing. We should treat self-love as the ultimate expression of love and true happiness.

We live in a state of scarcity, have a need for control, and develop a mental disposition that forces us to live with a lack of understanding, sometimes succumbing to destructive habits and living in denial. We just sit and wait for the right man, the good job, the great vacation, the surgery, or the lottery win. Such emotions have caused us to react to environmental stimuli and observe behavior changes in others. We often learn to lose our autonomy, to deny our individual rights, and to leave our responsibility to ourselves and others; our honor is missing and replaced with disassociation and self-preservation. When we are weak, other people can manipulate us, leading us to feel unworthy of other people's love. To maintain integrity or survive in slack waters, we settle for relationships in which one person plays the role of tormentor and the other the martyr, silently responsible for carrying the burden of suffering.

How can we love someone we don't even know, respect, or cherish? Nobody simply throws away a precious treasure, but can we call ourselves a true, valuable, and unique treasure if we don't truly know and love our own self? Without self-love, we are strangers to our innermost desires, passions, wants, and needs. We struggle with low confidence, feel self-conscious and inferior, and are constantly indecisive and extremely anxious. Life becomes a series of tragedies, and we feel like we're stuck in traffic, going nowhere. We value our ego's selfish purposes over all other things and all other people. Or perhaps we construct walls that separate us from the real joys of love, intimacy, and relationships. Generosity, compassion, kindness, selflessness, and open-mindedness are characteristics we don't possess.

### 2.1. Importance of Self-Love

It is important to understand the distinction between self-worth and our identity. Your identity is an alignment of the highest, most perfect version of your true self, the God you have within you, the breath of life, the divine power, the unlimited truthful potential for love and happiness and abundance, and the unlimited creative capacity that lives within each of us. Your identity is perfectly you and not someone else's delivery of you. When you attach the concept of your identity to your understanding of your self-worth, to make changes, you seek external validation from the people who live in the world outside you.

Numerous psychological, spiritual, and personal development programs are evidence that people are only fully able to address the fulfilling of their dreams if they are prepared to love themselves the way they are. By doing so, they offer an enormous gift to the world. This unacceptable number of people is a reflection of how people see and judge their own worth. It is a critical moment for most of us worthy to reflect on our collective understanding of this topic.

Many people seek perfection outside themselves, but the change they seek is within them. Global statistics tell a story of poor self-worth. They say that 85% of the world's population suffers from unkind self-judgment issues caused by low self-worth. Low self-worth is the source of all pain and suffering that human beings experience. Having low self-worth is similar to trying to drive a car without petrol; it won't work. You are the engine and petrol of your dreams, and your self-worth is the dedicated petrol that gives life to your dreams.

*2.2. Benefits of Practicing Self-Love*

One of the greatest results is that we simply feel peace. We no longer fear what others think about us or whether we will unexpectedly lose everything we have. When we practice self-love, we move through the course of our lives confidently and lovingly because we know that our worth is absolute. When we no longer fear loss, we embrace our authentic selves and invite joy into our daily lives. Our true selves, our lives are brimming with opportunities to utilize our greatest gifts. The world then reflects those qualities back at us in an abundant display of love and living. We count ourselves lucky in life, and we find the world to be a love-filled, wondrous place.

When we practice self-love, we become an incredibly powerful person. We offer the world our best because we feel good about who we are and what we stand for. We are more optimistic, more appreciative, and more respectful toward others. As a result, our relationships become stronger and healthier. We embrace bravery, growth, and creativity rather than hiding away, settling for less, and feeling stuck. We focus on our health, which means that we feel our best on a daily basis and can be of greater help to others. We express our authentic selves, so we achieve our full potential and accomplish our deepest dreams. Without a doubt, self-love is a gift that continues to give and give. When we value ourselves as worthy people, we make better choices, are more effective communicators, and become powerful leaders in our personal and professional lives. We are happier, healthier, and lead more fulfilling lives.

# CHAPTER 3

# Cultivating Self-Love

Get to know yourself and believe in your talent. Connect and interact with different parts of yourself. Engage your five senses, visualize your dream future, and through visualization, feel how you will look, behave, and think. What do you see and think? What do you do with the freedom and money? What do you hear and say? Some people might find it easy to do this self-exploration exercise, and for others, their limiting beliefs, fears, and self-doubts might not let them visualize their dream life clearly and effortlessly. Therefore, in the meantime, please set your intention to become bolder, open to opportunities, resilient, assertive, confident, and grateful for the opportunities and challenges that come your way and make you stronger.

Cultivating self-love: 5 practices and habits for overcoming rejection, accepting who you are, and embracing your true worth. How do you cultivate self-love? Our self-love revolution journey has shown that self-acceptance, coming out of hiding, and joy are key aspects of self-love. Supporting and nurturing our well-being and healthy ego are as well. In this post, we will look at some other tips, practices, and habits to help you with your self-care journey and make it easier, enjoyable, and more effective. If you'd like a shorter self-love journey summary, it's available in the 4 Self-Love Tips to Help You Embrace Your True Worth video episode.

### 3.1. Accepting Yourself Unconditionally

Do you love yourself that way? Most likely, that's one of your main goals in life, right? My purpose is to help you become unconditional. I'm better at dealing with self-content, so that's where I can help you. My goal is to help you as you try to deal with self-acceptance so those personal responsibilities that tend to prevent personal love do not ensnare you. That way, you won't feel disappointment, and you will feel capable of feeling love for yourself and relating to others. For many people, though, that sounds like something impossible, especially when most of the time, you don't even like what you see reflected in the mirror. How do I put that into practice when self-love or self-acceptance is so far from my day-to-day reality? Most of the time, the solution to overcoming this feeling of incapacity is to realize that how you love yourself is something you can choose to believe in or not, but it's really just a decision. You create your own reality.

Can you honestly say that you feel love for yourself unconditionally? All the time? Regardless of what you look like, what you've done or not done, said or not said, thought or not thought? Self-love means being able to feel love for yourself, regardless of your actions, thoughts, appearance, emotions, or anything else. It means being able to accept yourself completely, in each and every moment, without conditions. It means believing that you are okay, and that you are worthy of love, regardless of your actions or the positions or titles you hold in life.

### 3.2. Nurturing Self-Care Practices

Methods: In this qualitative study, we recruited a diverse sample of Mexican American women aged 18–23 to participate in focus groups. Women were eligible to participate if they self-identified as both Mexican and American and reported having at least one family member who was born in Mexico. This population represented the second generation of the largest U.S. ethnic minority group. Researchers conducted six ninety-minute sessions. The first author served as the facilitator and a co-facilitator, graduate and undergraduate students trained in qualitative research, recorded discussions. Sessions were held in English in a large university setting. During discussions, participants identified components of self-love, generated themes related to self-love, and created a model of self-love. Transcript data analysis was completed in NVivo 12 and via a constructivist approach to thematic coding analysis.

Nurturing self-care practices: Making self-care a conscious act. The connotation of self-care practices is that they are inherently treats, a reward for hard work. Since these practices are not perceived in society as unrealistic, we often neglect them in times prior to burnout and injury, thinking only about ourselves when things become desperate. This attitude does not treat self-care for what it should be: joyful. A conscious practice that fully cares for our body and mind varies significantly depending on an individual's lifestyle. To begin to dive deeper, we turn to the examples of the delicate forms of physical, mental, and emotional self-care that this may involve. Regaining self-confidence involves self-care in all areas of life. Particularly the area of nurturing your mind which then makes your spirit sparkle.

### 3.3. Setting Boundaries for Healthy Relationships

We cannot have healthy relationships with others until we have a thriving relationship with ourselves. No, it is not selfish to love ourselves; it is essential. Yes, it is possible for us to walk as individuals and love one another. There is balance in the two. The truth that we are all unique individuals with our own separate life paths as well as "I love you", "I protect you", and "I make no harsh criticisms but only of love". Those two belong together. Setting those boundaries honors and respects us as well as the other person. It says, "I love you, (our) relationship, and myself." If you make it a boundary, the relationship will reflect love, humility and respect, not codependency, control, disrespect and fear. Let us put selfishness aside and shelter some self-love. How do we turn to ourselves? We honor ourselves. We respect ourselves. We protect ourselves. We love ourselves — first and foremost. We never let boundaries dissolve or disappear because they never made us their masters.

Falling in love with ourselves and embracing our true self-worth is such an amazing accomplishment. It is inner peace, love, and gratitude toward ourselves. It is pure joy, serenity, vulnerability, and courage. It is freedom. It is the greatest sense of accomplishment and empowerment we will ever feel in our lives. And of all the revolutionary skills you will ever experience and learn to master, finding ourselves, loving, respecting, and honoring our true worth are the most essential of all.

# CHAPTER 4

# Embracing Your True Worth

For many, our sense of worthiness is tied to our net worth. 80% of Americans have some form of non-mortgage debt, and some remain in debt because they see it as a symbol of identity or social acceptance. However, our worth is not defined by our credit score or job. Deservingness is not dependent on what we can do, become, or achieve. Realizing the truth about our worthiness - that it is an integral part of who we are - can help us understand that we are enough as we are. Therefore, it is important to take the time to recognize and honor our worth. Start by examining your early relationship with money and consider where your beliefs about value come from. Reflect on your childhood and early social conditioning. How was worth and deservingness defined in your family?

A 2019 survey found that 47% of Americans are uncomfortable talking about money. This discomfort can negatively impact an individual's financial life and lead to silence when facing money issues. It can also perpetuate behaviors that are not beneficial. The first step in transforming your relationship with money is understanding how the mind works, particularly in terms of self-love. Self-love starts with recognizing your worth. Worthiness is inherent and has been with you since birth. Society has influenced our perception of worthiness based on gender, and we often compare ourselves to these standards.

### 4.1. Recognizing and Celebrating Your Strengths

You may think there "aren't any" traits or skills that are truly good about you, as people have told you that you are awkward and ugly since early childhood. You couldn't dream of being able to help other people succeed academically, find inner peace, beauty, and security in themselves. Still, you actually already possess teaching wisdom and have empathy. You possess the ability to uplift others. Others discover it in you, and you still don't. Sound familiar? Time to unveil your strengths!

What's risky about this? Why don't we do this naturally? For many reasons! Socially, we are told that we should not brag or think too highly of ourselves. We may be scared of others' reactions when they hear about our strengths. What if they don't like or even hate us because we're different? Recognizing one's strengths also means acknowledging what we want from life and leaving behind what others expect of us. Finally, many of us have learned to stand in our own way and stop trying to achieve more. Insecurity intervenes, stopping us from ever taking full advantage of our strengths. And all the while, instead of getting to know our true worth, we focus on our own shortcomings and convince ourselves of our inferiority. Understanding and valuing your strengths isn't a child's play, but it's the most amazing adventure in a person's lifetime.

One of the hardest struggles we face is recognizing and accepting our own strengths and realizing that those traits make us valuable. To embrace your true worth, you first have to consciously recognize that you possess strengths at all and that they're what make you special. Then you learn to accept and celebrate them. As we do that, we start to see that our strengths can play a valuable role in the world and our lives. Recognizing and valuing our strengths leads to self-appreciation, which is a foundation of self-esteem.

### 4.2. Overcoming Self-Doubt and Negative Self-Talk

Practice cognitive restructuring. This involves replacing negative thoughts with positive ones. You will notice four times in your day when negative thoughts can take over. Before you go to bed, when your brain has time to unwind and overthink every situation, when you wake up, and then after breakfast. During these times, replace your negative thoughts with uplifting ones. Throughout the day, take time to catch any negative thoughts you may have. Take a break and find something you enjoy to take your mind off things. Negative self-talk is someone else's opinion that stopped in your head. Find its source, and why it does not agree with you. Ignoring the opinions of those you do not respect is crucial to taking your power back. By addressing these four low points in your day, you will diminish the self-doubt that constantly bombards you. Be patient. It is a process to overcome low self-esteem, with many small victories. Positive thoughts are powerful. Fill your head with empowering ones, and you will start to see lasting change set in your life.

Overcoming self-doubt and negative self-talk. One of the severest causes of low self-esteem is negative self-talk. When we constantly tell ourselves that we are not good enough, over time, we begin to believe it. This leads to anxiety, depression, eating disorders, and self-destructive behavior, and overwhelming perfectionism. The first step in overcoming negative self-talk is learning how to recognize it. The second step is learning how to fight it. The most powerful strategy is understanding the link between our thoughts and our emotions. The way we think creates the way we feel. If the focus of your thoughts is negative, then your emotions and outlook on the world and yourself become dire. Understanding this is the first step in recognizing and fighting off the habit of negativity.

### 4.3. Building a Positive Self-Image

4.3.1. Changing Self-Image isn't Easy. It has actually been proven through research that people with low self-esteem usually become triggered by the other than more selfish behavior, which doesn't mean that those who suffer from low self-empathy are in the wrong, it just means that such individuals have a history that is wounding their empathy. This can sometimes make you feel eerily self; it can feel like nothing else exists except your self-talk, but rest assured that you are only lucky to be ignored by your fears and insecurities. Your fears might have success in appearing powerful, yelling negative garbage into your ear, but you are actually hollow inside; you are a good person made up of a unique spark.

Acquiring a history-making self-image is not something that we can do overnight. You are not going to wake up tomorrow and suddenly love everything about yourself. But you didn't wake up today and despise everything about yourself either. This mindset has been instilled in you over time. These lovely negative beliefs have been ground into your day after day and are so familiar to you that you hardly hear them anymore. Changing a self-image is not about a quick fix, it is about being diligent bit by bit over time. As Richard Brandt points out, self-image is a tiny wisp of a thing. It is a fragile, precious creature and it needs constant attention, love, and reassurance. Do your best to be kind and patient with your self-growth.

### 4.4. Pursuing Your Passions and Goals

Prioritize your life choices. What you do is genuinely meaningful and not just to fulfill some person's artificial standard. Living as a reflection of real happiness, not a predictable gauntlet of random pursuits, is our resounding statement of worth to the world: "I am important, and I deserve to be content." Pursue activities enjoyed because they are activities of love. They increase the endorphin levels and release feel-good hormones. Furthermore, they both dull the memory of pain and offer a way of breaking through the intense emotions. Many people use diversion as a method of handling the everyday strain. People often find that in practicing the regular ritual of the skill, they become a little less challenging over time. If you are dissatisfied, spend time on things that give you happiness. In doing so, you create joy, success, and personal growth. Another fringe advantage in releasing any negativity stored up inside you is that along the way, you avow your value.

Many people have chased after others' ideas of "success" for fear that their own wants and ideas were not adequate. To live with self-love and joy, you need to chase your own dreams. Passion is infectious and throws a glow on everyone who is near it. Are you content when you find yourself talking about activities in your life? Do you use them as a yardstick? If you are not savoring them, life could be passing by. Create goals that fascinate you and pursue them. Without a passion, you cannot dream. Without a dream, what reduces your life to an everyday routine? When was the last time you felt you experienced something special? Mihaly Csikszentmihalyi created a term: "flow" is the mental state where a person in a state of operation is fully immersed in a feeling of energized focus, full involvement, and success in the process of the activity. In essence, he contends that life satisfaction is to be found in the pursuit of things that grow and stifle what burdens you. You have the ability to design these tasks to match your strengths and be swaddled. It is paramount to find something you enjoy and proffers that opportunity.